The Mole XI NWP

The Mole XI NWP

Poetry and Jazz in Dancing Shoes (A Triptych)

Ron Raye

New Wave Publications

CONTENTS

CONTENTS

CONTENTS

CONTENTS

CONTENTS

Also, by Ron Raye

Stories

The Intruder
Stories
Ms. Ballywit and the Editor

Novels

Witches Brew (Book I)
Witches Brew (Book II)
Witches Brew (Book III)
Witches Brew (Book IV)
The Red House
Maelstrom

Caribbean Quintet (Vol I)
Caribbean Quintet (Vol II)
Caribbean Quintet (Vol III)
Caribbean Quintet (Vol IV.)
Caribbean Quintet (Vol V)
A Cascade of Flowers
A Breach of Trust
The Final Curtain
Don't Wake Me in the Morning
The Shut Out

Poetry

A Discourse on Language
Open Seasons with Roxianne More
Just Off Colloden Road
In the Heart of Summer's Birth
A Cry of Voices from Backward Streets
Metaphor on a Jazz Slope: Song of the Sweet Dreamer
End of the World
Island Under the Sea
The Happy and Tragic Life of an Ordinary Citizen

The Mole (Vol I)
The Mole (Vol II)
The Mole (Vol III)
The Mole (Vol IV)
The Mole (Vol V)
The Mole (Vol VI)
The Mole (Vol VII)
The Mole Vol (VIII)
The Mole (Vol IX)
The Mole (Vol X)
The Mole (Vol XI)

Published by New Wave Publications

First Printing

Library of Congress Cataloging-in-Publication

The Mole Vol XI.:Poetry and Jazz in Dancing Shoes (A Triptych)/Ron Raye
ISBN: 9798988264453

1. Poetry

Printed in the United Kingdom

1

The Mole Vol XI.: Poetry and Jazz in Dancing Shoes (A Triptych)

Ron Raye

2

I Walk Around with Poetry in my Head

I

The day has begun with bursting sunlight.
It settles in the park
and in the trees.
Dogs become happy and start to bark.
It shines all day.
Through it glows our right to exist.

I walk around with poetry in my head
wild metaphors and incantations.
I can't sleep steady on the bed
A phrase or an image wakes me
always at the stroke of midnight.
It's hard to get back to sleep.

When you are cursed with the pen
and always searching for that elusive phrase,
Poetry comes at strange times of the day.
It tickles when you are depressed.
It remains about you twenty-four hours.
The soul of it I must caress.

But with you, it will not occupy the grave.
It's driven to search for another soul
to possess. That is worthy
of the name or the will to take the man
into the alley of virtue and peace.
But with you, it will not occupy the grave.

Poetry is the family you love,
the grandchildren you spoil with honey, sweets,
and hugs. The ones that will occupy your will.
They are fresh and warm in your arms
and take you back to those dark days in the womb
now that you will return a child's laughter.

It takes you back there with a peaceful spirit,
and you are out of this chaos with a smile
that transports you to other worlds you don't
recall. But those worlds are always waiting.
Poetry becomes your lover in all
things new and in all reflective images.

4

Through the darkness, it speeds
up, eating leaves
before the hungry insects set in.
I am the autumn leaf that kisses your shadow.
I wait until the morning breaks
then, kissing the earth are the snowflakes

The long drag of life wears you down.
There is a point at which you cannot go on.
Now, you wear the compromising crown.
In your armor, you discover a crack
a conglomerate of images ensure
that writing poetry will bring you back,

and will perhaps make life more livable.
The world and all its trappings will come to pass
after you and all your siblings are gone
There will be no more need to wear the mask.
You will no longer be a pawn
in someone else's convoluted game.

5

Through the darkness, it speeds
up, eating leaves
before the hungry insects set in.
From destruction, they compose poetry
and feel no staring eyes among the dead.
They have put life's deadly toxins to bed.

The world opens its doors to you and all.
One suspects hoping you will fall
and keep this aging world
at your back. You'll make the silence yours
Through the darkness, it speaks.
Let me follow you in the throes.

Out of this glorious life, I wait
for the ugly kindness of death.
It comes to me with a deceptive solitude
and I accept reluctantly,
but I go into his loving arms
and surprisingly, there were no alarms.

6

I am off to find other worlds.
Now, it has begun with bursting sunlight.
Out of the clouds, a ghost emerged,
drifting across the old universe
as the dirt of us waited to be purged.
I kept telling them that life was a curse.

But nobody listened to me. I had
better be talking to myself. I sat
back and watched the proceedings unfold.
I am no prophet, and I don't want people
to think I am above all else.
On the contrary, I am like everyone.

Else. I struggle with the oddities of life.
I am subjected to abuse like everyone else.
I am often faced with those who think they
Have a handle on life when most of us
are in the dark about what we see and hear.
We don't know how to fight despair.

7

Through the darkness, it speeds
eating leaves
holding on to the bare threads of life
or whatever is left of it.
This life is a sprawling landscape of poetry
like a lamb munching on grapes in Coventry.

None of us will let go until the very end
and that's poetry, too, the fight for life
visit the sick and give them comfort
poetry in all life is what, why, and when
and all the amenities we take for granted.
Carve out a life to accommodate your mood.

Perhaps we'll find ourselves back here again
living a life of which we have no memory.
Through the darkness, it speeds
eating leaves.
So, in destruction, the cycle begins
and, at some point, we all become bereaved.

8

In retrospect, we could have done better.
I mean living life without the hate.
Be the last letter in the alphabet
for all of it, I mean the awkward angles
that scuttled along the coral reefs
the waves and all that watch us sleep.

It is poetry, all of it. Life escapes
the vault of secrecy, the open-air
of all that is new.
We have drunk the pages of history
becoming drunk, refusing to see the truth
that rolls from its metamorphic tongue.

We cry the tears of poetry in sadness; in grief, they drink the wine of sorrow.
Such things from poetry you can borrow
when life is filled with joy; you give them back.
Complete whatever you set out to do.
Yesterday, you know, I won't stay on the rack.

9

Conclusions will breathe you in tomorrow.
Today will give you what you need to complete
life, perhaps there is no completion of life
It's a cycle that we return to measuring
ourselves in bits and pieces of time.
It's the burden of the rhyme that confines

And make us what we are,
that troubling night between death and light.
It might well be something lodged in our hearts;
Something bothers me on this season's flight
and was never meant to be extracted.
For you, I open the nature of poetry.

It tickles the bottom of your feet
and gives the caesura time to heal.
This alliteration of the dead
holds you hostage under the weight of words.
The images are swimming in my purse.
Poetry makes sense of the madness of the times.

10

Write it at night and in your sleep.
Know this: you can't pay for life in rhymes.
Everything you have gone through, you will keep.
Among apparitions, I see you
working your way toward me
between us exist is eternity.

Against the burning sea of light
slept my gift for employing alliteration
and making the sentence dance.
There was always, in my work, nothing but delight
and execution of the word puts me in a trance.
Poetry is the movement of jazz.

Sounds of the saxophone and piano,
the clarinet expands flowers of joy.
The drums awaken you with sweet rhythms
Vocal caresses you in soft romance.
Poetry is jazz, and jazz is poetry.
It moves to a rhythm outside of time.

11

Through the night, you are obliged to wander.
Towards me, an apparition that you
recognize for out of the night so much
sweetness lingers of jasmine and oleander.
In your hair from youth, your hair is still intact,
all luscious and vibrant. I see you smile.

And I understand why. Life has been good to you
and poetry is a matter for all concerned
building on the joyous splendor of truth.
One doesn't argue if life is good
how in anger when things are going wrong.
But keep the rhythm of your song,

and I was on my way, then I saw him
in the season end and the autumn coming,
to grab you from the jaws of death's claws
and visit with sharp eyes what's within you
that truth nobody's willing to see.
One must cut through bits and pieces of metaphors.

12

Carve them up as a surgeon would then put each
piece under a microscope. You will observe
the diversity of words dancing,
asking for the uniformity
of time to look within itself. O life,
let me be the shadow of what you are

Or what you were before the world exploded
into creation. I was alive yet dead
to the unseen horrors of what has been
created. And when the devil convened.
We saw the clarity of our iniquities
like a glass of water serving as a mirror,

ourselves reflected there. We saw the dirt
and wished that we were all clean.
Yet, by the Hand of God, it seemed
that we would all take the world
down for the count, and in its state,
that was not what man wanted. Or was it?

13

Nobody knows. It was the last time.
He saw himself in the mirror. He waits,
but there is not even a smile. You greet the world.
Somebody will return that greeting.
Fame, desire, and lust don't go seeking.
Then, there was the voice and an ominous sign.

Of rain clouds. One should see life as incantations
that never stops but keeps changing,
transforming life into triple objects.
It is the world as it becomes you.
I touch you with the summer wing of myself.
I touched you with the summer wing of myself.

Take me into that world, that sign of sweet angels
where it rains silver and gold.
I stand in the shower, waiting. I see
you for both of us, waiting is eternity
and I was you, and you were me.
I lay my body across the grass.

Bursting sunlight
bold and brave under the sun with my eyes
open. Let me poll you into my fold,
for I dream sweetly or sweetly dream
that you were constantly quivering about
corridors sniffling my cologne

Sweetly, it intoxicates me.
And ever since, I have been eating at it
Like wood ants eating the inside of a tree
trying to get the true essence of taste.
And I am sitting on the fence again
reading the poetry of myself in death

A sweetly constructed phrase brought me back.

The day has begun with bursting sunlight.
It settles in the park
and in the trees.
The dogs became happy and began to bark.
The sun shines all day,
and through it, it shows our right to exist.

The origin of the poem is unknown
Does it come from the head?
Does it come from the heart?
One can hardly tell if what I said
comes from an alignment with the stars.
It may just be the poet's inconsistent hands.

14

One does not understand
the source of literary mystery.
In the face of twilight, it sings poetry,
and we are once together again.
I pull you reluctantly from the picture frame
and grasp your trembling heart.

The day has begun with bursting sunlight.
It settles in the park
and in the trees.
Dogs become happy and start to bark.
The sun shines all-day
and through it, our right to exist.

The origin of the poem is unknown
Does it come from the head?
Does it come from the heart?
One can hardly tell if what is said
comes from an alignment with the stars.
It may just be the poet's inconsistent hands.

15

One does not understand
the source of literary mystery.
In the face of twilight, it sings poetry,
and we are once together again.
I pulled you reluctantly from the picture frame
and grasp your trembling heart.

The day has begun with bursting sunlight.
It settles in the park
and in the trees.
Dogs become happy and start to bark.
It shines all-day
and through it grows our right to exist.

The day has begun with bursting sunlight.
It settles in the park
and in the trees.
Dogs become happy and start to bark.
It shines all-day
and through it grows our right to exist.

16

You can find a poem while circling the block
and when the sun goes down
listen to your voice; every image a rock
and you, the metaphor clowns
alliteration gives way to endings that dance
to bells at rolling Christmas, the last chance.

In a second, life came before me
I sing the songs of all
and I see your facc.
Perhaps it's the muse and its grace.
I toppled before your infatuating time.
Once more, the silent lover of flowery rhyme

Let me walk straight into you
at the slow pace
of old age. This is poetry you can't see.
It happens at any time of the day,
even in the corridors of despair.
Walking in the colorful city center

17

Is the tongue of poetry
the voice of seeing everything
that others don't or never see.
Let me pass
for I am as
brittle as glass.

I shall come again,
and I will meet you
Once more, there are neither doors nor
windows in that other world.
Before you, the smoke of life will curl
upward. But it will come down again.

We are here now, and so is poetry
that presents itself before us wrapped
in elusive images to be decoded.
In the metaphor, the image is trapped,
hoping for a way out
and with passion I shout

18

I am in love with you.
I crossed the threshold on top of the burning mountain
to write a line to define you who inflamed
my loins, poetry is outside watching us.
If death holds forth his hand, take it
he will not abandon you in hours of sleep.

The day has begun with bursting sunlight.
It settles in the park
and in the trees.
Dogs become happy and start to bark.
It shines all day like a star.
Through it glows, our right to exist.

The mountains stand still
in the shadows of the trees.
People should resist the urge to kill
each other. It would help if you existed
on the essence of peace
About this, I speak with the deceased.

19

The consensus is that it should be so
I hold my fist up against all wars.
Destruction is the sickness of men.
His ego is the shadow of all hate, and on top of that, he seals his fate.
The mountains glanced back at you with a smile.

I stand only in silence, listening to nature speak.
I look into her eyes and see
nothing but the joy of a sweet solace.
I have become the keeper of time.
Your life in its uncertainty is rhyme.

Without a regular pattern
I calculate the angles of the sunlight,
and with my net, I drag it through the clouds.
The earth was spinning
while I cleaned the linen.
Life is without a pattern.

20

When it all began to fall apart.
I mean the earth's axis. It was all rusted
and we thought it was salvageable.
But it was all busted
and beyond repair
the poor feller was there lying on its side.

The mechanical engineer stood looking
in bewilderment. He could not understand
the construction. It was like nothing he
had ever seen. It was a poetic meltdown,
an apocalyptic nightmare that kept
us awake all night. The moon, in its sympathy, wept.

I shall come again,
and I will meet you.
Once more, there are neither doors nor
windows in that other world.
Before you, the snake of life will curl
upward, but it will fall again.

21

And hope will return
following the collapse of everything else.
Poetry becomes tragic without fulfillment
in that hour not of you
I won't go on without it. I mean love
I must bombard you with honesty and truth.

You carry the ball without fumbling,
without taking life for granted. But I'll wait
I am not only hoping that you'll come.
I am also hoping that you'll stay.
Let the world pass.
I won't come back.

But don't you sleep in regret
fall back against you.
I am composing something now,
and I put you in the frame.
Will you remain till eternity.
I grasp the shadow chasing you.

22

But I can't hold on to it.
I can't fix whatever went wrong.
I can patch you up, but it won't hold.
This patch is like life, temporary,
and you'll go on singing the same song.
By then, your host will be gone.

The origin of the poem is in me
and I measure it in phrases and images.
Look, I have a metaphor for you
it's wrapped in chrysanthemums
all designed for you in the caesura
splitting hairs with the simile.

I am the poet who lives on the road.
I came home with dust in my eyes
and the world far behind me.
But I am alive and promise to love you again.
At night, I'll watch while you sleep and compose
words in a complicated frame

23

Please remember that I am no sage
filled with wisdom.
I fell so many times.
I can't keep count.
On my way out, I can hardly see, but
my faculties are still intact for nights

Let me wake up and find you next to me.
They tell me you walked out of the abyss.
Your whole generation is almost gone,
and mine? One can hardly find a trace.
Time swooped them up in one gulp.
He takes no prisoners.

Time is your shadow of death
and shining still are all those who are dead
breathing new lives
into all those who are gone.
The mountains stand still
in the shadow of the trees

24

I am the poet who lives to cast a spell
on any who would succumb.
Who will death take next? I cannot tell.
Only that I live in a dream
that has multiple interpretations.
I can't tell you what dreams are.

But it's enough to know that I have
been captured by the enemy
brainwashed and tied in chains
from day to day
I sing of better days to come.

I live in the washed-out hours
of what is to come
the sliding back of time
catches us lacking in one way or another.
Neither you nor I can tell
the life of others and ours is not secure.

25

We die in songs every day
and can barely detect the effect
time has on us.
It goes like a cat scampering across the grass.
We all succumb to it
until we become brittle like frozen glass.

Perhaps we'll find ourselves back here again
with nothing to live for, only that
it's a changed world
and now we are a rift of smoke that curls
recklessly upwards. Nights, we cannot see
the golden hour of the sun erects in its stance.

We follow the sympathizers
sleeping outside under the trees
protecting against war because it leads
to pockets of poverty and suffering
and confirms the moral decay of democracy.
Sleeping sweetly are the deceased

26

Through the darkness, it speeds
up, eating leaves
before the hungry insects set in.
I am the autumn leaf that kisses your shadow.
I wait until the morning breaks,
then kiss the earth with the snowflakes.
The origin of the poem is unknown.
Does it come from the heart?
Does it come from the head?
One can hardly tell if what is said
comes from an alignment with the stars.
It may just be the poet's inconsistent hands.

I don't know, and I suspect neither do you.
With you, I gather my things,
but I don't run. I wait until you shed tears.
I am not all for despair.
Only the metaphor in which you wrap yourself.
I peel it apart with my image.

27

I come singing to you with nothing at my feet.
I see you for these nights I do not sleep.
I wander around in the living room
thinking of things to come
and not for a moment, I assume
that you won't come back.

Your presence tossed in a dream.
I had of you and wake up in joy.
Seeing your face extracts me from sorrow.
The caesura I employed for your
alliteration is the face of tomorrow.
I gauge my love for truth.

Poetry wakes me at midnight.
And I, a loyal servant, answer his nudge.
Nothing else I can do but play his game.
His world's not heavy. It's light,
and I was not at all searching for fame.
I wait for the sun to show its face through the rain.

28

I walk around with poetry in my head
wild metaphors and incantations.
I can't sleep steady on the bed.
A phrase or an image wakes me
always at the stroke of midnight.
It's hard to get back to sleep.

Sometimes poetry is a hack job
of jumbling words pasted together to make sense.
One must always make sense of a clause
awkwardly placed in the sentence.
But life is often untidy like that
in mid-sentence, one can't turn back.

One must fully construct the phrase
for poetry is cut and paste
Like a sort of world pastiche of another world.
One must fully complete the phrase
for poetry is a complicated face
that is sometimes difficult to formulate

29

The day has begun with bursting sunlight.
It settles in the park
and in the trees.
Dogs become happy and begin to bark.
It shines all-day
through it glows our right to exist.

I cry with the yellow tulips at my back.
The hibiscus emerges from your hair
to welcome me under the summer sun.
In me, you won't find any dismay.
For I am the poetry of your soul.
I am the star providing you with fun.

In my heart, there is a strange silence.
You wait for me at the gate.
I am trapped in love's tremors.
But if you come at the appointed time,
I promise I won't be late
for time dances between us.

30

I can take you on my journey,
for I follow the poetry of the time
and the night without rhyme
I give you the sweetness of eternity.
In the end, poetry will no doubt kill me.
But to me, it matters little.

I move towards the heavens,
thinking that I am sweet upon you.
I am the poetry of time and rhyme,
the follower of complicated wordplay
that comes back to the heart of you;
thinking of you, I become happy and gay.

I am the poet who lives on the road
for summer is upon us. I see you
in myself. Your angel, am I.
You light up the sky like a simile
that smiles for its survival.
I keep you for life is with me

31

You are no longer here
So, there is no point in me hanging around
there is nothing left but space
and for all of me, your grace
your voice, by the sound
is missing from so far away,

and into the distance, I remember you
from this or that, I see you as myself
asleep at night, wraps me in a spider's web.
I am there for the duration to kiss you
and feel myself gathering before you.
Poetry becomes the joy of laughter.

I am laughing again
stand there with flowers in my hand.
Your favorite bouquet of tulips
for you to place in water and think of me
asleep, you remain in my dreams.
I am laughing again.

32

To see you in all your glory,
I came back from this.
So, In my heart, there is a strange silence
of you waiting for me at the gate.
I bring you chrysanthemums.
Let's begin a clean slate.

I follow you home like your shadow
close to you all the way,
smiling with your jasmine perfume.
I cherish what you have given me.
Stir and inflamed me like a youth
open to all things about love.

For you, I sing in poetry above the night.
You sit on the stars
with nothing else but life before you
under the trees, there are no leaves
but I sing of you always
in the light of the glorious sun

33

When there are no more shadows left
for us to follow, our existence will have ceased
and still active will be that evil rift
among men, and so at heart will be the quarrels
the destruction that brings us to our knees.
I value that open face against the clouds.

The landscape and all its burnt offerings
give us our peaceful beginnings, and then
we smothered what was to begin in laughter.
Now, in all the chaos, we know nothing of ourselves.
The sun comes down to us without anything.
I give you all that is nothing within you.

I fight to breed hate against all wars
and create hot rain to melt all weapons
create protest groups to cease the march
toward conflict and nuclear build-up.
I am not into a sweet rhetorical flare
that leads to the destruction of civilization

34

And the disappearance of communities.
I fight to breed hate against all wars
and live beneath the tulips of silence.
I am the angel who fights against political
corruption and the suicide of living comforts
for the poor. I am the angel for the working poor.

For justice and peace, I open the door.
I sit atop the mountain, watching the plague
of the poor orchestrated by political maneuvering.
There is the feeble mind that dwindles
before our very eyes. The night doesn't wait.
Politics corrupt the body of life.

I fight to breed hate against all wars
and create hot rain to melt all weapons
create protest groups to cease the march
toward conflict and nuclear build up.
I am not into sweet, historical flare
that leads to the destruction of civilization.

35

I fight to breed hate against all wars
I fight to eliminate the causes of war
Justice for all is the elimination of conflict.
I live in the master of myself and populate
comfort among people with low incomes.
These days, I sleep on the floor.

The day has begun with bursting sunlight.
It settles in the park
and in the trees
dogs become happy and begin to bark
the sun shines all-day
and through it, our right to exist.

I have gone over to everything else.
I am the master of myself in the hope
that you will wish me well.
I'd wait and be willing to sell you
what I have taken from you
the sale of time all belongs to me

36

As well as you. For you belong to me.
I wait for you in the essence of myself.
Hold that over me. Shut the windows to all
things new. I walked on, watching you
in all your splendor.
The joy of laughter lives within the soul of man.

I won't slap you. The earth is on its last leg
a journey that wishes you out of yourself.
I have been wrapping around the silence
of what is not and what is.
Now, you can understand the state of things.

I walk around with poetry in my head
wild metaphors and incantations.
I can't sleep steady on the bed.
A phrase or an image wakes me
always at the stroke of midnight.
It's hard to get back to sleep.

37

You are the curse in my dreams
the lover in my blood, it seems
that all is not well.
The world will tell
you something new, and nothing will be unique.
Dogs believe in a simple bark.

I suppose there is nothing at that window.
Only the night that the sky sings
of times past and the world that fades before us
and comes back again to see us repeat our deeds.
ominous in the air, there is something
evil driving us toward the dirty waves

that drive us back into the drifting debris
the insidious images we see while
on the dive; dirty things we see in men's hearts
I took the A train there
I mean, up to the stars
then down again and got off at Central Park

38

Where Bill Evans played.
I could not sleep until he finished his set
and out of the blue came Ahmad Jamal
a scintillating finger spin on piano rep
that surged through the silence of the night
left me smelling the dancing hibiscus.

I give you Thelonious Monk moving mountains back
breaking all the rules
and still carrying his tune.
he's a breakaway pleasure of the night
a man who pounded the piano back in tune
out of tradition, he took flight

and, I may add, created his tradition
falling side to side, up and down
until the music comes into tonal consistency
with all that went before it
At midway, a piece can be fixed
and he makes life a smooth sound.

39

The day has begun with bursting sunlight.
It settles in the park
and in the trees.
Dogs become happy and begin to bark.
It shines all-day
through it glows our right to exist.

This day I see you forty years
from now, and you remain the same.
I hold you up to the sparkling light
and you refused to play that game
where life becomes an intruder of despair
and everything turns out to be clickbait.

Life, my friend, is plagued with deception;
it infiltrates every corner that you
can't see around. It lays dormant until
one becomes vulnerable and alone.
Then, outside the experimental world
something or someone molds you into a clone.

40

I gathered my belongings and bid goodbye,
Not even observing the summer sky.
I hold my hands up to you
and follow you through the rules
that fall below the horizon of the truth
will confine you to everything substantial.

I am the voice of what poetry is.
I am the grass, the mountains, and the sea
through poetry; I worship you. Give the world.
Nothing but you. I walked into the sunset
with nothing else but me. Substantial
burns in every object I see, a metaphor

Rolling itself toward me. I pretend
to be a star sliding across the sky,
an angel coming to push you into the folds,
Of the skies. I kiss you, then say amen
to all my brothers silently kissing me.
I open the window to let the sunlight in.

41

The day began with bursting sunlight
It settles in the park
and in the trees.
Dogs become happy and start to bark.
It shines all-day
through it glows our right to exist.

Through the darkness, it speaks,
eating leaves
before the hungry insects set in.
I am the autumn leaf that kisses your shadow.
I wait until the morning breaks.
Then, kissing the earth are the snowflakes.

I walk around with poetry in my head
wild metaphors and incantations.
I can't sleep steady in the bed;
a phrase or image wakes me
always at the strike of midnight.
It's hard to get back to sleep.

42

Across the river, I saw you
shadow in a yellow dress
I came, and you, I bless
with the summer hibiscus
its petals warm fall to the earth
waiting for another birth.

This is my sextet of ice cream
that last until winter.
You are the vanilla that caresses the stars.
I wanted you to whisper something
before eternity wrapped us in its embrace.
I am intoxicated with your grace.

I solely came to you in love for all
of you without anything else but
the world and the chaos within.
I wait for in silence
coming to you I may fall.
But I will get up and keep coming.

43

I fight to breed hate against all wars
a fight to eliminate the causes of war
Justice for all is the elimination of conflict.
I live in the master of myself and populate
comfort among the poor.
These days, I sleep on the floor.

A cascade of autumn leaves tells us nothing.
More will fall the next season
and that the winter comes on
the hurricane will get intense.
But I won't turn back. I will come and get you just the same
to live with passion is not wrong.

I sat there drinking lemonade
listening to Duke Ellington's,
This One's for Blanton
Bass – Ray Brown
Do Nothing till you hear from me
the Duke follows you through eternity.

44

Up next was T. Monk
pounding on the black and whites
fingers coated with velvet gloves,
pounding out his intro
he remained *alone in San Francisco – from 1959*
you see him riding shotgun in his trench coat

on a San Francisco streetcar
heading into the heart of happiness
having the time of his life.
Jazz becomes the joy of peace
and the life source of all beginnings
jazz, its unusual rhythm follows you home.

That summer of sixty-three
I remember pretty well
each other; we were sweet.
We lay stretched out on the carpet,
kissing and listening to noisy Cicados.
Then I slipped on *Interplay* (1963) Bill Evans

45

Guitarist – Jim Hall
He'd play throughout as though he possessed
not a false note, for he had the call.
Bass – Percy Heath
was nothing but a rolling sweet.
Drummer – Philly Joe Jones

It was a steady and substantial stone.
His brush strokes were soft, punctuated
with finesse. Two thin jade bones
laughing, controlling the rhythm of the song.
Trumpet – Freddie Hubbard's
rendition of, *You, The Night, and the Music*

Jazz is the poetry of all time.
It dances and retracts on its rhymes
leaving room for stretching tones
Rhythms come back to haunt us in sweet
melodies. Musical arrangements
open avenues for new and fresh suites,

46

The origin of the poem is unknown.
Does it come from the head?
Does it come from the heart?
One can hardly tell if what is said
comes from an alignment with the stars.
It may just be the poet's inconsistent hands.

If You Like, Get Hold of This One: Helen Humes,
In the forties.
Married Man Blues
Drive me Daddy
Blues Ain't Nothing But a Woman
The poetic landscape begins here.

In healthy love and despair,
I saw them
They all walked the tightrope
gathering the songs of time past.
But we hear all those
voices through the glass.

47

Willy Dixon
Jump Jackson – Drums
Memphis Jake – piano.
Terry and McGee
T-Bone Wallace – guitar
They go on until eternity

Back there
Helen Hume's- *I Cried for You*

Jazz is the poetry of all time.
It dances and retracts on its rhymes
Leaving room for stretching tones.
Rhythms come back to haunt us in sweet
melodies. Musical arrangements
open avenues for new and fresh suites.

Through the darkness, it speeds
up, eating leaves
before the hungry insects set in.
From destruction, they compose poetry
and feel no staring eyes among the dead.
They have put life's deadly toxins to bed.

48

Drawn to the sweet light of sound,
There is always rhythm beyond time
but life is uncertain, complex, and long.
Our cut-off point is the moment before time stops,
which is the silence of our death.
But jazz, in its immortal state, goes on.

Beyond the despair and happiness of things
about the rumblings of life, I sing.
I will go with you inside the harmonica,
and I stayed there counting the notes
that instrument with its unique sound
carries the warmth of jazz's overcoat.

The passage of jazz wraps itself in memory.
In death, we forget yet remember nothing
but darkness. Nothing can go beyond
that unseen image. Only life if it
comes back through that mysterious flash
and again adorn us with bitter, sweet pleasures.

49

He was backstage dancing to bebop,
having a fabulous time,
and all of this after a once thriving business flopped.
Life wasn't going to beat him down.
After all, he had all that jazz
and he could play an instrument or two.

Nothing was going to smear his parade with shit
Jazz was a back poster child
and in its lap, with an instrument, he could always sit
in laughter and praise.
once, I saw him playing the saxophone
in a jazz club north of Pendleton Street.

He was all laughter and giggles.
They said he took the jazz world
by storm. Then, to him, a twin was born.
Twenty years later,
they also took the jazz world by its horns.
Jazz, I say, remains the poetry of all time.

50

It dances and retracts on its rhymes,
leaving room for stretching tones.
Rhythms come back to haunt us in sweet
melodies. Musical arrangements
open avenues for new and fresh suites.
You hear it with the tongue of the wind.

Through the darkness, it speaks,
eating leaves
before the hungry insects set in.
From destruction, they composed poetry
and felt no staring eyes among the dead.
They have put life's deadly toxins to bed.

Poetry becomes the arc of life,
and shadows follow you in every way.
You have seen it. So have I.
Through the darkness, it goes
and jazz was, after time,
I popped in and saw him on the percussions.

51

He had a soft brush stroke
that tickled us; that brush had a balanced
tonal composure and a sense of place.
He went at it with grace
and had conversations with what he played.
He was a night overall.

Had the guitar dreaming rhythms
unto himself in that after shock of time.
He was himself and only unto himself.
He played as if God said something to him
that only he could understand.
He was the pause of time and music.

The origin of the poem is unknown.
Does it come from the head?
Does it come from the heart?
One can hardly tell if what is said
comes from an alignment with the stars.
It may just be the poet's fickle hands.

52

The hands that touch the breath of jazz
the sounds were sometimes allergic to grass.
Charlie Parker came through the night
with a *Night in Tunisia* – He blew
it, and it bounced back on us.
Then we heard *Laura*, a velvet sound.

That made women cry, thinking of past lovers.
Only Charlie could bring women to tears,
after which they could fight off despair
from broken love that sends them
into the bluest worlds with little hope
of coming out...

The day she had begun with bursting sunlight.
It settles in the park
and in the trees.
The dogs became happy and began to bark.
The sun shines all day.
Through it glows our right to exist.

53

Sunlight in the evening is the beginning of poetry
Mostly the start of a new day
Brings the fresh smell of flowers
I gather them for the evening
becomes flowers, and the jam session
that never ends – in jazz, you have a friend.

I shall come again with my song.
I will caress you with my rhythm
and let the angels sing
of new music to come
and on from years past
and I will see your image in the glass

From the memories of lives gone.
I heard the sound of his sax hissing,
kissing the twilight where women lift the skirt of the blues
in the grass with nothing else but mass.
The percussions were like a snake hissing
in the grass with nothing else but mass.

54

The origin of a poem happens in the moment
of your life when you understand less of life
and when you are living not even knowing
that you are alive. But poetry will be next to you
nudging you in a mysterious shadow
and fall away to let you create.

Poetry comes at you in moments of peace and turmoil
when the nature of existence is no longer understood,
and it would be best if you were forced to explain your purpose.
The world can't tell you what to look for; only create
a scene. Then, you can expand parameters
to include the soul of what music is.

I was at the end of Miles Davis's *Autumn Leaves*
when the hollow sound of his sax
blew me through a tunnel of endless worlds
from which I could not return.
That sound was as smooth as velvet.
The night wind blew back at us. But

55

the night wind belongs to Miles – the air
scattered with sound, and time goes on
in the battle of life returning
to haunt us with the saxophone melodies,
and his bohemian, sartorial elegance
adorn the stage with his sax phonology.

Tell me who is better. Johnny Hodges
with his mellow sound of intoxication
and his elegant serenades?
Give me Miles' *Love for Sale*.
He is even smoother in *Dancing in the Dark*.
You could listen all day sitting in the park.

Or smudge on your feet to the upbeat tempo
of our delight and If I Love Again
with Cannon Ball Adderley released
1958 twelve sounds on track
that sax had everyone's back
under it, nobody was going to crack.

56

I give you Clifford Brown and Max Roach
released in 1956 at Basin Street.
What's this thing Called Love,
Love is a many Splendor Thing
intersperse with jam sessions
is the real essence of jazz.

I fall in the sprinkling of autumn leaves.
Then, the soft echo of that saxophone
drifts through the wind with devoted consistency.
High and low softly on the tail of the wind.
He was riding on the wind alone.
His lover had deserted him.

We left the past behind us
and here again, autumn leaves are falling
and the voices are calling.
The wind is so soft and rising. A whisper
of a delicate stroke of the brush.
It crawls across the canvas,

57

I am falling aimlessly away toward the blessed.
Least feared in all this night
and all that before the night comes out.
I wait for the sails of the hour you blew away
yourself. It was the master of the alto sax,
Johnny Hodges, the night where jazz was soft.

Go to the window and catch what you can see
a whisper of music passing by.
It won't last for long. For long, it won't last.
This Aleen sound passes by once in a lifetime.
Somebody said it was jazz
and that it wakes the dead.

It gives one a purpose in life.
Get there fast and be with it; be fed.
Go to the window and catch what you can see.
A whisper of music passes by.
Outside now, the face of a face of eternity
wishes you well. Let jazz be your guide.

58

Into that world of the unknown
Johnny Hodges will be waiting for you
that smooth alto saxophonist
who delighted us with his velvet winds.
The soloist of The Sweet Night Winds
Feed your music desire with the New Orleans Suite.

Both of us were at the window, observing
the summer grass
and along came the winter
his huge shadow won't let us pass
and I wondered why.
I suppose a season has got some rights,

and if he comes around, he's not to blame
He's a facilitator of time,
a spiritual shower of rain
that thrust itself upon you when you least
expect it. He's the ghost of simple rhyme
and sometimes what hampers him is the beast.

59

He walks the earth singing praises to his
handlers. He's the joy of whatever he is
and sage of worldly things. Gracious
is he or he pretends to be of the night
belonging to him. He was of something else;
meaning all things belonging to life.

He kept outside of himself, his voice,
unfortunately, he had none – his function
was only a wish and that it was beyond
what we thought of him – it was Willem.
This feller was after something else.
We didn't know what it was. Neither was it the soul.

But he knew how to interact with us.
His social skills were top-notch with the women.
I don't mean that he was a playboy, and if
he was that he was after something.
What, nobody could say. Perhaps he
was offering a handful of joy and a cup of despair.

60

Go to the window and catch what you see
a whisper of music passing by.
It won't last for long. For long, it won't last.
This alien sound passes by once in a lifetime.
Somebody said it was jazz
and that it wakes the dead

Have them whizzing for life again.
It delights us into pleasure and happiness.
It's the spring and flowers of yesteryear.
That summer of yesterday, we were still
young and vibrant, waiting for the summer
to come again to whip us back into evil games.

He came to us in soft velvet nobody had ever seen
I did not want to intervene, and so be it,
and were it not for slavery back then
when the world had become undone. We parched
when stranded in the desert. Many came,
and we could hardly tell who they were.

61

The day she had begun with bursting sunlight.
It settled in the park
and in the trees.
The dogs became happy and began to bark.
The sun shines all day.
Through it glows our right to exist.

I give you this child of God
through the darkness, it speeds
eating leaves
before the hungry insects set in.
From destruction, they composed poetry
and feel no staring eyes among the dead.

They have put life's deadly toxins to bed;
and there is nothing more to be said.
Only the laughter of seeing oneself
tossed about in the wind like an old newspaper.
Then, it spat into a water gutter
and ended at a nondescript destination.

62

It's the shadow of all of us. An unknown
time warp that sends us backward. We heard
the children screaming and playboys scheming
when to life, we know there is little meaning
and life will continue to seem
perhaps we will not arrive at a definition.

But so, to speak, a cauldron of soldiers
making their way through the night
as though night had started somewhere
on a working plant that held us together.
We were down but not for the count, and in all
honesty history stayed with us.

I give you this child of God
through the darkness, it spreads
eating leaves.
Before the hungry insects set in.
From destruction they composed poetry
and feel no staring eyes among the dead

63

I would offer nothing less than Charlie Parker's Laura
caressing the air with his velvet sound.
They were yet fighting the demands of this life.
He was the hour, the silent hours
fighting his longing desires but

He was a bird of the night, a creature in flight
from something not of this world that was within
him. One can be sweet in a particular
way. But can succumb to the frivolous of pleasures.
Then, he was almost God-like
yet holding on to what made him what he is.

A god in his imagination and a belief
in what he was going to become.
What he hoped for was that everything
would belong to him and take him toward a world
of something else. It was all he came here for
A god was that of his imagination.

64

Both of us were at the window observing the
summer grass
and along came the winter
His huge shadow let us pass
and I wondered.
I suppose seasons have got some rights.

I'd be there, you know, like the wind in poetry
jazzing up how we look at the world.
Stay on the island retreat.
It won't help you in any way,
and you won't be able to lift that curse.
Don't be part of what's eating the world: deceit.

Go to the window and catch what you see,
a whisper of music passing by.
It won't last for long; it won't last for long.
This alien sound passes by once in a lifetime.
Somebody said it was jazz
and that it wakes the dead.

65

With its splendid rhythms and improvisations.
It had come along with scattered notes that
lifted the souls of men and set them upon
A path of serenity without looking back.
At times, in its confused and distorted state.
The way back only comes through that sound.

I mean the sound of Billy Strayhorn,
Take the A Train, the windows rattling
across the broad expanse of Queens
and with the sound, your smell of Harlem,
the outer edges of Manhattan
Eastside and Seventy-second Street.

Poetry becomes the arc of life,
and shadows follow you in every way.
You have seen it. So have I.
Through the darkness it goes
the sound of jazz was after him.
I popped in and saw him on the percussions.

66

I am the child who you think you are.
I walk in the shadow of the clarinet.
My father taught me. But I was no star.
I frequented the jazz clubs and alleys of Harlem.
That world was young and vibrant back then,
and you heard that saxophone from Miles away.

They would come together at some point. Jazz
and poetry, I mean. Their paths must have crossed.
That sound, it was impossible to pass.
It was intoxication on the soul.
Go back into that world, and you'll see.
It was sweet and full of complexity.

Both of us were at the window, observing
the summer grass
and along came the winter
His huge shadow won't let us pass
and I wondered why.
I suppose seasons have got some rights.

67

That summer of Nineteen-Seventy
was when I found poetry. I saw the face of Whitman.
This bearded bard opened the body of poetry.
His expansion of lines instilled in me
the possibilities of line endings.
He wrote powerfully into eternity.

The bard encompasses the whole of life.
He drags every line across the landscape
and hold it up against the light.
He showed the many faces of man
and saw in what he wrote man's crooked fate.
The bard encompasses the whole of life.

Through the darkness, it speeds
eating leaves
before the hungry insects set in.
From the destruction, they composed poetry
and feel no staring eyes among the dead

68

Once a blackish seal that closed the night,
I wait in silence to help the dead
and wish to God to take back things I said.
You were standing in the face of light
and though the light was bright, I could not see you
but the packets of dust were still present.

I'd longed to walk the earth like Christ,
feeding the hungry and preaching peace.
But for such things, someone would put a price
on your head. I wouldn't mind that you are
doing a good deed. These days, people don't read
much into showing a hand of kindness.

Go to the window and catch what you see
a whisper of music passing by.
It won't last for long; for long, it won't last.
This alien sound passes once in a lifetime.
Somebody said it was jazz
and that it wakes the dead.

69

I am the child who you think you are.
I walk in the shadow of the clarinet.
My father taught me, but I was no star.
I frequented the jazz clubs in Harlem.
That world was young and vibrant back then
and you heard the saxophone Miles away.

I stood outside the clubs listening to mostly
jam sessions that went on until morning.
And all the jazz greats were jamming and
stretching their instruments to the limit,
and I listened with great enthusiasm.
Of it all, I love the spirit.

Absorbing the variation in sound
and the skilled concoction in rhythm.
My memory created a reference
folder for all those sounds and sweet,
tonal arrangements. I did not miss a beat.
I found the true essence of art right here.

70

Through the darkness, it spreads,
eating leaves
before the hungry insects set in.
From destruction, they composed poetry
and felt no staring eyes among the dead.
They have put life's deadly toxins to bed.

Beyond the despair and happiness of things
about the rumblings of life is sing.
I will go with you inside the harmonica,
and I stayed there counting the notes,
that instrument with its unique sound
carries the warmth of jazz's overcoat.

Jazz becomes the arc and art of life
only into the sense of your rhythm
that time will choke you in its wake
and the night will break you down
then the music comes and soothes you
for this is the order of some truth.

71

In the sweet tones of a sound so flawless
was Hodges. He was the God of the alto saxophone.
He had it all in the marrow of the bone,
and he was a stone under fire with a desire
for perfection. Here he was, the sax talking.
His is a complicated fire.

The origin of a poem happens in the moment
of your life when you understand less of life
and when you are living not even knowing
that you are alive, but poetry will be next to you
nudging you in a mysterious shadow
and fall away to let you create.

I am the child you think you are; someday I will become a star
And you'll be able to see me from afar
and take me away from that disrupted park
about nothing. I call you out of the dark.
Johnny Hodges on alto sax.

72

Letting the nightfall away
into what was never going to be
what we expected.
It was never going to be a dancing delight
and nothing based on what we have read,
that we'll see the face of eternity

Making waves behind us, complaining
that he could see the world at large
and nothing but the sound of music
sloping on the dusty hours of a worn-out summer.
From music, you can spend your life abstaining
And even not remembering. But it lays dormant.

Both of us were at the window observing,
The summer grass
and along came the window.
His shadow won't let us pass,
and I wondered why.
I suppose seasons have got some rights.

73

The past is back to claim his pack
and he's not laughing
for the days have become so cracked.
Sometimes, nothing happens
only dead autumn leaves
that spend their lives recycling the earth.

In the dead of night, I see a reflection of myself
from which there was nothing of me.
Midway through life, I saw a fellow
who looked just like me.
We passed each other in the corridor
and neither of us dared to say hello.

I knew what you were thinking,
and you knew what I was thinking.
Together, we thought of one thing.
We won't die at the same time.
How are we going to say goodbye
thinking of it to my eyes bring tears.

74

Well, say, let the life we had
never be forgotten.
For people come and go.
But memories stay in the realm of shadows.
At dinner, we ate
in the presence of our own company.

I have been one with you.
Memories are formed from places.
We have been dropped into a new folder
entitled, Love
that folder could not be sealed,
for Love must remain open.

We must be able to get back in
Without any glitches
thinking about goodbyes
in such a sad way
but there was no despair
In such a manner that it was painful.

75

Go to the window and catch what you see.
A whisper of music passing by.
It won't last for long, and for long, it won't last.
This alien sound passes by once in a lifetime.
Somebody said it was jazz
and that it wakes the dead.

It is an open form like the free verse
in poetry; one also finds formality,
and its rhythms come together after exploring
tight jam sessions but holding steady
on a theme. It stretches out in all tempos.
I am waiting for you.

Finishes clean and tight, like a well-ironed shirt.
You come into your while following rhythms
that ask you to determine where they are going.
You can't sit still. One must be alert
to the variations taking place
you are, I mean your consciousness.

76

It is diverted to avenues where everything happens
even the dead will rise and go on in their
non-existent shadows – jazz is the breather
of time, it is the creation of tonal arrangements.
I hear the saxophone of the gods.
They take away the horror of despair.

The day had begun with bursting sunlight
It settled in the park
and in the trees.
Dogs become happy and began to bark
it shines all day.
Through it glows our right to exist.

Go to the window and catch what you see
a whisper of music passing by.
It won't last.
This alien sound passes by once in a lifetime.
Somebody said it was jazz
and that it wakes the dead.

77

Our philosophers will have a say in that.
But it does wake the dead,
and most of the time, it makes you clap.
This is a sign of happiness.
Many will tell you that
and all about jazz I have read.

I sit in the silence of time, waiting.
I shall go on despite your failing
soul before me. Let me see your face.
I don't, and I won't wait for despair.
It will surely wait for me.
I don't begrudge it that.

Let me stand up and be hacked
on my own time.
Let me construct my rhymes.
I am a sleeper of the harmonica.
I come before you
in kissing everything but you

78

The origin of a poem happens in the moment
of your life when you understand less of life
and when you are living not even knowing
that you are alive, but poetry will be next to you,
nudging you in a mysterious shadow
and fall away to let you create.

Jazz has floored me more than once.
I am soft in the stomach for the piano
and have a passion for the saxophone
but let them know that I am no clone
and that I create my sound.
I have baptized myself into the tone.

after which it's hard to go back
and search for time.
One can't say goodbye to jazz;
it stirs, and there is no point of decline.
It always sleeps in the heart of summer days.
To get in, there is a code you must crack.

79

And after that, there is no looking back
you have gone on into the realm of night
and day, night being the blues
and the day being the jam sessions.
From it all, you won't take flight.
It's only jazz, they all say.

I came across you, and I see the night
and wander into flight.
So forward I go and kiss the world.
But I don't peddle backward
with my saxophone, I grab the girl
and make way for the solitude of the blues

Through the darkness, it speeds
eating leaves
before the hungry insects set in.
From destruction, they compose poetry
and feel no staring eyes among the dead
they have put life's deadly toxins to bed.

80

The end was not near; jazz came.
Our way, and we had little say in it.
At the time, we did not seek fame.
The genes we cannot fix
and fate dies the same death
to that in a single breath.

I walk around with poetry in my head
wild metaphors and incantations.
I can't sleep steady on the bed.
A phrase or an image wakes me.
Always at the stroke of midnight.
It's hard to get back to sleep.

On this night, I saw my ghost,
and that non-entity was breathing hard.
Why, he was dancing to the music.
He had great moves, too, that old bard.
He had the slow and fast two-step going.
I tried, but I could not keep up with him.

81

Why, I swear, he was over one hundred years old.
I was ashamed, for I was half his age.
My ghost could play the clarinet
and offered to give me lessons. Refuse,
I could not. They were free of cost,
and nothing was lost to me.

He gave me his rendition of Caravan
and then disappeared like a puff of smoke
with no backbone, but he was gone just the same.
I did not fight with him. We were on speaking terms.
So, there was no bitterness between us.
We worked on the same side of the street.

I walked around with poetry in my head.
Wild metaphors and incantations.
I can't sleep steady on the bed.
A phrase or an image wakes me.
Always on the stroke of midnight.
It's hard to get back to sleep.

82

I held over until the summer came.
I'll paint the night with you
and never let go.
I was once the season of angels
and the summer leaves of poetry.
I threw myself before you but never asked.

It's time to catch your kisses.
I'll wait and sing with you
and follow you across the floor.
I gather all of you in the folds of my heart.
Stand with me, and I will sing to you.
I am the father living on one side of life.

The long drag of life wears you down.
There is a point at which you cannot go on.
Now, you wear the compromising crown.
In your armor, you discover a crack.
A conglomerate of images ensure
that writing poetry will bring you back.

83

But if you are honest with yourself.
At some point, instinct will tell you,
and indeed so, that you are a hack
simply trying to survive in a silly world.
Perhaps your task is for the good of all,
but ask them who will stab you in the back,

and then say hello; your life meant nothing.
Let's not forget that life is a dirty game
and can down you in many ways.
Living this life, everything is framed.
You mentioned that jazz will bring you back.
Why, who on earth can argue with that?

I have been taken by it myself.
Why, the alto sax is an instrument I have always loved.
But never learned to play it. I'd flip
on something new. Instead, I put on some stew
out of frustration of finding time
with me; I always had a knack for rhyme.

84

I walk around with poetry in my head
wild metaphors and incantations.
I can't sleep steady on the bed.
A phrase or an image wakes me
and always at the stroke of midnight.
It's hard to get back to sleep.

It's the haunting aspect of this life
trying to understand a process rooted in the spiritual and let it unfold.
It must. There should be no forcing the issue.
In life, one must try to get things right
you must be comprehensively bold

In executing your task. Don't turn back
and never leave the job unfinished.
It's always a race toward a finished
that one never sees coming.
It's in the make-up of the map of life,
and you find yourself always running.

85

I remember that summer; it was so hot
that not even a glass of lemonade
could quench my thirst. The clouds let the sun out
deliberately upon us. He knew.
I mean the clouds, that it would be the hottest.
The day the orange was heavy-handed,

and there was nowhere to hide.
Then I heard the autumn leaves, Cannonball Adderly,
from the album, *Something Else*, 1958
recorded at the Van Gelder Studios,
featuring Cannonball Adderly on
alto sax – Miles Davis (trumpet) softly

as they came, Miles was, his sound was as soft as velvet
Hank Jones – piano
where the rhythm continuously flowed through
the room like stars dancing to a strange rhythm
a woman I kissed once remembered called me
and asked if I was still listening to jazz.

86

87

Sam Jones – bass
Art Blakey – Drums
then I am to, *I Cried for You*,
Count Basie and Helen Humes
Buddy Difranco – clarinetist
Freddie Green – guitarist.

Wardell Gray – tenor solo.
Let your soul warm up to *Blues for Madelin*
Johnny Hodges – alto sax and
Bill Davies – organ
Jimmy Hamilton – clarinet.
Sit back and let the joy of jazz pull you in.

The day has begun with bursting sunlight.
It settles in the park
and in the trees.
Dogs become happy and start to bark.
It shines all day like a star.

Through it glows our right to exist.

88

I am back to listening to the sound
of Duke Ellington and Jimmy Hodges.
Passionflower and *Black Beauty*
Performed on piano by Ellington.
I am moving on to *A Love Affair*.
Performed on guitar by West Montgomery,

a pure pleasure to listen to – golden fingers
with a velvet touch that leaves you soft inside.
The rhythm holds you and won't let go.
It comes in the afternoon and asks you
to dance; tell me, who doesn't like the rhythm
of a jam session? I put it to you.

that creation is one massive jazz session,
and continue to be in the making
that complicated walk-through existence
that puzzles both you and I, to our rescue
comes jazz, it's the burning, complex task
that, I assure you, never will last.

89

The origin of the poem is unknown.
Does it come from the head?
Does it come from the heart?
One can hardly tell if what is said
comes from an alignment with the stars.
It may just be the poet's inconsistent hands.

I walk around with poetry in my head.
Wild metaphors and incantations.
I can't sleep steady on the bed.
A phrase or an image wakes me
always at the stroke of midnight.
It's hard to get back to sleep.

And we shall dance in the hope
of bringing life to those who shall
remain nameless in these troubled times
where nothing comes back to haunt us.
We always remember ourselves
following nights before the joy of what was.

90

We cried the tears of poetry in sadness
and grief, then drank the wine of sorrow.
So thin us from poetry you can borrow.
When life is filled with joy, you give them back.
You can do whatever you set out to do.
Yesterday, you know, won't stay on the rack.
Conclusions will breathe you in tomorrow.

The night before that, I heard the sound of jazz
outside. It came from far away, I thought.
But it was under the window the sound of crickets
at twilight in the Caribbean, insects
dancing to the sound of the waves crawling
toward shore, and the insects answered.

Without knowledge of itself, the world ambles along
like a lazy summer day, a song
filled with despair and happiness
and I must, however, ashamed I am to confess,
that there was no bitterness in me
about something I love but did not understand

91

Love, a piano playing, Monk in the living room
that joy with laughter never ends.
I will drink with you a cup of tea and soon
we begin to dance like two young lovers
and you, a daunting, pretty girl
with curious eyes, unaware of the world.
It will entice you to some mysterious end.
Then, give way to happiness and charm.
At every phase, you will think of her as a friend.
But be cautious; she can be volatile.
Let wisdom be the parting gift of time
and patience be the magic of our style.

Love, a trumpet plays Miles in Central Park.
Birds asleep awake to find themselves in tears.
The sound of the trumpet goes to the heart.
One finds no room for despair.
Only in the silence of the room there is a voice
that will drown noises out except the trumpet.

92

Love is the night that wears itself thin.
It knows how to make you laugh.
Sometimes, you shed tears that can last forever.
It puts millions of flowers in your path.
At times, you fall into the dance of sin
and worship the pleasures of the heart.

Through the darkness, it speeds
eating leaves
Before the hungry insects set in.
I am the autumn leaf that kisses your shadow.
I wait until the morning breaks.
Then, the snowflakes kiss the earth.

Love remains a pair of dice;
one never knows what one will get.
On Monday, you get rice; on Tuesday, you may get a kiss.
But one may also receive lots of heartache.
Then, slowly, one's heart begins to close

93

Death waits patiently in a corner.
His appointment book has space
for everyone.
He is devoid of prejudice
and welcomes you despite your iniquities.
It's a dining room where friends gather.

To talk about old times. We all suffer
from the same affliction.
Unfortunately, none of us can go back.
The road back is sadly burning
and over us, the constellations
are awkwardly turning.

Here Comes Love Again

The long drag of life wears you down.
There is a point at which you cannot go on.
Now you wear the compromising crown
in your armor you discover a crack
a conglomerate of images ensure
that writing poetry will bring you back

94

95

And I am at it again, working toward you
but I don't know what to expect.
All coming to you is nothing but truth.
I have walked around the arc of love.
We stand under the awning, and it's raining
with love, we started framing

It was when the summer threw its light on us.
You can't hold anything back,
for love is an umbrella hovering over us.
We can't hide from it. Neither can we hide from love.
We must, despite suspicions, interact
without being afraid to take a chance.

We cry the tears of poetry in sadness
and grief. Then, drink the wine of sorrow.
Subtle things from poetry you can borrow.
When life is filled with joy, you give them back.
Complete whatever you set out to do.
Yesterday, I am afraid, won't stay on the rack.

96

Yesterday will take a bite at tomorrow
and let you know where love is hiding,
but it won't let you know which direction sorrow
we'll be travelling. I, love will show you.
For I am a loyal friend. Ask the kiss of peace.
Remember, time is not here for you tomorrow.

To all those who are willing to die
to eliminate all wars
to throw ideologies and allegiances to the side
and kick on with enticing neutralities.
We want to get on with it
and leave the world within itself.

Life is the night that wears itself thin
it knows how to make you laugh.
Sometimes you shed tears that can last forever.
It puts millions in your path.
At times you fall into the dance of sin
and worships the pleasures of the heart.

97

Tonight, the weather is terrible. There is thunder.
The hurricane has toppled everything.
Some people come out to steal and plunder.
Perhaps life is meant to destroy man
and send him back to the age of stone.
But he'll have to stand on his fragile bones.

To all those who love life, come with me
and I'll take you to the House of Angels,
where they will give everlasting life.
Awaiting you will be eternity;
bc carcful not to lct it fall from your hands.
It's only life, but it will bite you sometimes.

Get Johnny Hodges, *Texas Blues*
on Verve *Small Sessions* 1956-1961
Hodges is a dream on alto sax
while listening, I was drinking milk.
His sax was like gulls flying over the Atlantic
clean, fresh, and reminds you of touching silk.

100

I could not turn back now.
I remember we made love while
listening to Johnny Hodges:
A Flower is a Lonesome Thing.
The beauty in her eyes sparkled
and, in my memory, is still perfumed.
She was the angel when I could sing.

And joy be me, and joy be you.
All others that went before you
were passing glances.
But you were the permanent star of the night
and the angel that makes me dream
that from you, I'll never take flight.

Through the darkness, it speeds
eating leaves
Before the hungry insects set in.
From destruction, they composed poetry,
and feel no staring eyes among the dead.
They have put life's deadly toxins to bed.

101

I have heard the noise of the screws.
I will wait for you to reach home so that we can dance
to *Bye Bye Blues*
featuring:
Muddy Waters
Memphis Slim, Willy Dixon.

After the music finished, we are still dancing.
It is poetry, all of it; life escapes
the vault of secrecy – the open-air
of all that is new.
We have drunk the pages of history
becoming drunk, refusing to see the truth

That rolls from its metaphoric tongue.
Then, out of the blue, she wanted to hear
T-Bone Walker and his famous guitar riffs.
Luckily, I have some of his work�
and I was more than happy to bring it out.
There was no fallout between us.

102

I walk around with poetry in my head
wild metaphors and incantations.
I can't sleep steady on the bed.
A phrase or image wakes me.
Always at the stroke of midnight,
and it's hard to get back to sleep.

Shadow in a yellow dress
I came, and you, I bless
with the summer hibiscus
its petals, warm, fall to the earth,
waiting for another birth
waiting for another delivery.

The window is open because autumn is upon us
and I have dusted the sheets.
I welcome you back to a house devoid of dust.
I want to experience you dreaming in sleep.
You and I together, God willed it so.
How can I go against His Word?

103

Shadow in a yellow dress.
I came, and you, I bless
with the summer hibiscus
its petals, warm, fall to the earth,
waiting for another birth.
And we may say that it's a curse.

But we sing in rhythm with life
and it always turns out to be this game
you and I have been playing
for so long that life is not understood through it.
I know that there are people who have no interest in fame
and that our society is plagued with ills.

After poetry, the world holds itself
together, and that phase of music comes again.
Here, men drink the joy of laughter,
and nothing is ever the same again.
There is always the flight of time
that never comes back.

104

Poetry becomes the kingdom of the known.
Sometimes, the unknown
never sleeps. Only remains in the bones.
Dormant, waiting to be awakened by the night,
and then the practicality of day intrudes,
takes it by the hand and leads it somewhere.

Poetry and jazz are not separate genres.
They are the same.
The simile, metaphor, and caesura
all came from the same variation
of metrical wordplay
none of them will cause you any despair.

I walk around with poetry in my head
wild metaphors and incantations.
I can't sleep steady on the bed;
a phrase or image wakes me,
and always at the stroke of midnight.
It's hard to get back to sleep.

105

I never say farewell to the seasons,
For like them, you'll be back again,
and I will kiss you once more
together we'll play on the floor
like children laughing with and at the world,
but then you were always the girl.

One never learns why one
is placed on this earth,
even after living a lifetime.
Ours turned out to be a random birth.
It's the simple business of living
and the noble company of giving.

Poetry and jazz are not separate genres
They are the same.
The simile, metaphor, and caesura.
All come from the same variation
Of metrical wordplay
none of them will cause you any despair.

106

Eventually, one finds oneself back here.
Only death would be yours with a smiling face.
It's in your living room,
and I'll make you mine with grace.
Because life is all but a balloon
waiting to be pierced. It's simply a mass of gas.

It was all there to see life, it's cruelty
always leaves one hoping to get through it,
and it will never take the same road,
an unpredictable experience
fighting its way back to decipher the code
that spread the secrets across the ocean floor.

You all should know that I am not
the body of myself
but the hope of another generation to come.
I'd be moving cautiously under the sun
and I'd gather all my time and sleep
only leaving the children to weep.

107

A Digression Cycle

II.

108

I.

From the world, it cuts you off
In its warm and unintrusive hour,
silent in its engagement and fickle cough.
You never see him coming, but he sits in his tower.

2.

laughing, watching his shadow work
Like a serpent sleeping in the grass.
He creeps up on you and bites you in the ass.
Then you go back to sleep in a corner of your purse.

3.

The pleasure of listening to you
is like observing the constellation.
It is so varied and silky in its beauty through and through.
Not a note is struck wrong.
You are in the heart of creation.
Go with God and the angels and do
what the end of life dictates.
A song remains in the teary eye of fate.

109

4.

The Voice

I am the resistant shadow to all oppression
and the protesters to all political corruption.
I am the guillotine that slices up iniquities
and the sword that beheads you
for leading the vulnerable
into poverty and disenfranchisement.
I am intolerant of deceit and greed,
I am the voice that, in the end,
It will make you suffer and bleed.

Sitting in my room
drinking tea one evening,
he called on me, and I replied: Why so soon?
Aren't you going to let me pack?
Not even a pair of underwear?
Why, my body has been ravaged by age.
Let me cover my scars
and I'll be on my way.

110

I could die now and be done with it.
But that would be cheating you of something owed,
a lifetime of happiness,
even if life does not promise such a thing.
But if you are complacent and pompous,
Fate will rob and scam you of everything.

6.

Come back to me.
I am tired of being alone.
What I want badly is your kiss.
Let me crawl through the marrow of your bone.
There is nothing at all amiss
about wanting you.

7.

Come back to me.
I am waiting in the park
on that same bench where we first met
pounding still is my heart.
My eyes are forever wet
with tears that fall like rain.
Sometimes, love brings
with it lots of happiness. At other times, pain

111

8.

Come back to me.
I am tired of being alone.
What I want badly is your kiss.
Let me crawl through the marrow of your bone.
There is nothing at all amiss
about wanting you

9.

The pleasure of listening to you
is like observing the constellation.
It is so varied and silky in its beauty through and through.
Not a note is struck wrong.
You are the heart of creation.
Go with God and the angels and do
what the end of life dictates.
A song remains in the teary eye of fate.

10.

I walk around with poetry in my head
wild metaphors and incantations.
I can't sleep steady on the bed
A phrase or an image wakes me.
It's always at the stroke of midnight,
and it's hard to get back to sleep.

112

11.

I come to you once more
singing the joys of life
where your kisses begin to cut me in pieces.
Is there any recourse from the shower
of your kisses?
Come back to me. I want to win you again.

12.

I come upon you as the loss of me.
Outside the bees feed on the chrysanthemums
while I dream of you.
In the silence of myself.
Let us finish beyond all else.

113

III.

Beyond this, I know the world
as happen stance beyond you
and it would be best if you then held yourself upright
I shall come to you in the summer
but shall I have in winter?
And will this no longer be love?

Death, unfortunately, has just arrived.
But I am not ready yet.
I have not put my house in order,
and I am still washed and drowned in regrets
about my life decisions.
I am not yet prepared to take that deep dive.

I am leaving so many unanswered questions.
I turned to jazz to find the rhythm in
the mystery of death. Nothing comes less
than when you encounter that beast within.
Listen, sweet Ahmad Jamal's Autumn Leaves
Ahmad Jamal on Piano

114

James Commack, contrabass-Double bass
Alphin Riley – Batterie drums calling the night wind
Manolo Badrena – percussions – a badass.
Who pushes the envelope into other worlds?
Jamal, with his velvet fingers, sings
himself into hearts of autumn leaves.

It cuts you off
from the world in its warm and unintrusive hour.
Silent in its engagement and fickle cough,
you never see him coming, for he sits in his tower.

Laughing, watching his shadow work
like a serpent sleeping in the grass.
He creeps up on you and bites you in the ass.
Then you go back to sleep in a corner of your purse.

115

116

One can open oneself up to the night
and light against the ugly claws of life.
But nothing is guaranteed to bring you delight.
On one's way to work, one may kick a stone
that doesn't move or blink an eye.
Such small things are bad luck. You are not alone.

Put your faith in what will come through the skies.
Things crumble like sedimentary rock.
But life keeps on forging a path.
Keep up or render yourself a block
that cannot from life extract
a giggle or a laugh.

I go deep into the darkness with you.
There are mysterious voices we cannot discern.
Next to me, I can hear your heart throbbing.
one cannot get over love at a moment's notice.
From the inside, the world is rotting.
We are here holding it together.

117

In the end, everything collapses,
and we are left in the balance.
I go deep into the darkness with you.
But I was unable to see.
Nothing can rescue us.
Not even eternity.

We are the evil of what we are
and the burden of every star.
For each of us, a space is vacant,
and in it is our resting place.
It will always be waiting there
behind all else, the moonlight slips.

All men die without knowing.
Our lives are stricken with the burden
of uselessness, wandering about aimlessly.
We have suddenly stopped growing,
but love is always in a state of coming back.
There is no reason to sit and wait for the glass to crack.

118

Death, unfortunately, has just arrived.
But I am not ready yet.
I have not put my house in order,
and I am still drowning in regrets
of my life decisions.
I am not yet prepared to take that deep dive.

But love must follow, however depressing the state
of life. Those days of pleasure are a burden,
for our actions contribute to our fate.
To forgive despite pain is the measure
of a man's character and virtue.
It's the hour of blooming chrysanthemums.

It's the season of open summer youth.
You, sometimes, find yourself back in time.
But it's usually not for long
because we survive on singing the same song.
The pleasure of hearing the voices of children
and the music of my slow demise

119

Eventually, one finds oneself back here.
Only death would be yours with a smiling face.
Sit in your living room,
and I make you mine with grace
because life is all but a balloon
waiting to be pierced by a pin. Life is an explosion.

Shadow in a yellow dress.
I came, and you I bless.
with the summer hibiscus
its petals warm, fall to the earth
waiting for another birth
is life a curse?

I never knew what it was
for life to blossom every day.
Sometimes, it brings happiness and despair
and leads us into the sound of waves.
Nothing holds us to the death of time
but the rhythmic jazz rhyme.

120

We are the evil of what we are
and the burden of every star.
For each of us, space is vacant,
and in it, our resting place.
It will always be waiting there
behind all else, the moonlight slips.

121

The Art of Writing

124

Shoot Straight

125

126

Shoot straight, and you'll hit the lizard's tails,
my mom used to say. But she was shot dead
from an accurate one that ricocheted,
proving that one can't know which side of the bed.
Death prefers to cast his silent hour.
With the imagination, God plays tricks.

His metaphors bounce off the towers,
and like a dark and poisonous shrimp pricked
us into creation, his master plan
which, sadly, is neither here nor there.
But a platform on which the grotesque stands
mimicking the voice of a world once here,
Double helix in two hologram shows.
You remembered your shadow the night before.
The demons came and tugged at your leg.
But you were already wrapped in folds of snow.
Let the hurricane come. It won't last long.
The sun will sweep it away in one swipe.
But life will always come back to haunt us.

127

Against the Demons

128

Well, what I have seen now from the pulpit
came the arrival of my wicked self
Where I make time to confess
the indifference of my behavior
toward all those who hold me in contempt
complacent, yes. But not a heart of stone.
I am blessed with a frame of fragile bones.
Guilty, I plead, but my heart is soft like a sponge.
Mine is not a heart of bitterness.
Now I crouch in your closet like a moth.
Instead, it would seem that multiple landscapes of my dreams
are harvesting consolation
from deceptive demons who plague the earth.
Guilty, I plead, but, like a sponge, my heart is soft.
Now, I crouch in your closet like a moth.
Poetry wakes me at midnight,
and I, a loyal servant, answer his nudge.
Nothing else I can do but play his game.
His world is not heavy. It's light.
I was not at all searching for fame.
I wait for the sun guides its face through the rain.

129

The day began with bursting sunlight
it settles in the park
and in the trees.
Dogs become happy and start to bark.
The sun shines all day.
Through it glows our right to exist.

At what price will we sell our souls
to occupy the house of fame.
It's short-lived, and we all know.

130

Clarinet

III.

131

Because of love, it was easy for me
to arrange the taste buds on the palate
and break the barrier.

I remember resisting at first
because I like meat thoroughly cooked
eating half-cooked dishes was like a curse.

But once the spell is liked, one returns
accepting the natural order of things
days spent with you become blankets of verse
because of love, I have flown into unknown
waters plagued with enemy mines and tongues
hostile and discriminatory to the bone.

Once I smelled the flowers in your hair
those sweet tentacles that haunt my soul
and, like a rag, dragged along by the waves.
Because I am unsure of where the current ends,
I drifted while love held me hostage.
My palate's ambiguities extend.

Beyond a caress, the night of a kiss
I dig deep into the liquid world of myself.
Twice, I held you unable to dismiss
Then, I thought that all of this would last.
But now sweet days the present presents
It discourages me from living in the past

I held out so long that when you came
along, I got trapped in a two--
dimensional world – A three-world glass frame.

132

Intermission

133

We keep playing this game
that does little to help our cause.
We breathe the night of madness.
There is always a clarinet in the attic
and I have seen it from every angle.
The world as we see it is walking still.

But the forest is dark.
Again, the day has begun with bursting sunlight.
We come and make our mark.
But we are no stars.
I don't pretend to know
being the life of all that is.

Through the darkness, it speeds
up, eating leaves
before the hungry insects set in.
From destruction, they compose poetry.
And feel no staring eyes among the dead.
They have put life's deadly toxins to bed.

134

I held myself upright
A blast of pride disgusted
under shades of delight
a history map of the Trojan horse
entwine with the battle of drops of blood and bleeds
in defense of this howling voice.
Nothing significant was said.
I have entered you with a shield and sword.
The world went wrong. Now, man is dead.

The origin of the poem is unknown.
Does it come from the heart?
Does it come from the head?
One can hardly tell if what is said
comes from an alignment with the stars.
It may just be the poet's fickle hands.

You can find a poem while circling the block
and when the sun goes down,
listen to your voice; every image is a rock
and you, the metaphor crowns
alliteration gives way to ending that dance
to bells at rolling Christmas, the last chance

135

Let me pass
for ai am as
brittle as glass.
There is a shadow
lingering on the underpass
He's been thrown away because of class.

For him, they did not cut a path.
He licks his wounds
and sets off for the underpass.
But it doesn't bring him
any solace.
He's all alone.

Inside that body of night,
one could see
the bodies in flight
a child dead by nightfall.
The leaves of autumn scattered
throughout the universe.

136

137

138

But I would miss the last dance,
which always seems that night
would come for me first. No chance
of me outliving you. Do I have the right
to let you wander into that dark alone?
But we don't choose fate. It chooses us.
At what price will we sell our souls
to occupy the house of fame?
It's short-lived, and we know that.
Nobody is to blame
if the world goes up in flames.
That's what we tell ourselves.

Let me pass,
for I am as
brittle as glass.
Is there a shadow?
That lingers below the underpass.
He's been thrown away because of class.

139

I am the settling night of you.
Let me throw a kiss
and if you feel it gives a catch
work your way around the edges
of life, be cautious, for life is fickle
and can jump you at any time.

Learn to trim your hedges
and be in unison with nature.
Don't let the world pass you by.
In old age, God sometimes is kind.
But you don't know it.
In the end, you'll see his face.

He'll reveal his secret to you.
You fall beside me and softly I sleep
to dream and dream again for in you is truth.
In me, I promise there is no deceit.
I come to you with a warm heart.
I have open windows, of you I am a part.

140

Gather yourself – make the mark.
I'll be waiting, waiting when death has done its work.
At that moment, I wait
I listen to your laughter
and the tide in your stride.
I follow you with everything.

The day has begun with bursting sunlight.
It settles in the park
and in the trees.
Dogs become happy and begin to bark.
The sun shines all day.
Through it glows our right to exist.

Who can know what death is like
Without experiencing it?
You can't explain it to anyone.
It remains a mysterious flip.
It's a complicated song.
That you never hear again.

141

It lives in a frozen world of its own,
just like the strange rhythms of a jazz quartet.
It approaches you in different moods.
But you must sweetly accept it,
for you will never see the night coming.
You'll remember the summer ice cream cones.

What you did to enhance your lover
cannot always turn life on its head.
Always there is thunder and rain.
Eventually, one must have a chat with the dead
And forget the lovers of fame
one must strive to be a giver.

We are the evil of what we are
and the burden of every star.
For each of us, a space is vacant,
and in it is our resting place.
It will always be waiting there.
Behind all else, the moonlight slips.

142

I don't know what it is
But I have been waiting here.
Not for anyone.
Only to see what joys life will
bring me, if any at all.
But I know that in death, I'll still be

waiting until the angels sing
I already know that no bells will ring,
and that the sweet ends of summer will cling
to the worn-out end of your skirt.
I know already what is there.
I mean in your heart's comfort.

I am not all you want in this life.
Neither am I all you desire.
But I am the angel who watches over you
and the shadow you see in your dreams
I am the Coletrane of *Giant Steps*
I try my best not to make you upset.

143

I go in search of he who mistook you for something else
Man lives his life without knowing the essence of it
and at the hour when life is a brute.
He jumps back and rides his hour upon the flute
at a distance, you always see the trick.
But the game is always in the time of youth.

Where the evil of what we are
and the burden of every star.
From birth, we hope for the good of all things.
But life sometimes has its hand in a sling
rise from the ashes and hear the birds sing
to survive on earth, water is everything.

Let the elements be your only guide.
The night win will warm you with its chill.
Now and then, a man is bound to slide.
Life doesn't destroy you. But only nature will
and she will always outlive you.
But come back into the fold, please do.

144

In the autumn silence, I have grown
to love your hair in a single strand of it.
I discovered the marrow of my bone
and in that secret joy of a switch
I let your voice, like a flute, drift on
like curls of smoke that fades,

into another dream, another utopia
that promises to wait out those burning
end of days that will never make their way
into time, the unseen.
Or what you aspire to be
that rising, elusive star

That feeds itself with the desires of youth.
Pour into me your youthful and refreshing dreams
like water from a faucet, I soaked up
the details of every plan like a sponge.
I am all ready to take the plunge
into alternative forms of expression.

145

I walk around with poetry in my head
wild metaphors and incantations.
I can't sleep steady on the bed;
a phrase or an image wakes me.
Always at the stroke of midnight.
It's hard to get back to sleep.

At that hour when life falls dead
one must try to rise again
never become confined to bed
impossible in life to escape the pain.
Life was created with measures in place
to go sweetly into the night with grace.

Yesterday, I suspect, will be tomorrow's friend.
And today, father of the present.
He's much to say about our rotten past.
We can only do one thing but descend
and observe that deceptive shadow cast
itself upon the conscience of the past.

146

Live in the shadow of what you are
if night casts you aside,
find comfort in the stars.
Sometimes, people up and die.
There is no mystery to it,
for mortality is the human curse.
It can't be lifted
with the silver from your purse.

My objective as a writer is
to relish every sentence I write
and make people feel something.
One must see the world in a different light
however ugly and sinister.
One must fight for another view

Of the world. Everybody knows what is there.
But confronting things you cannot see
is a straight line to the face of despair.
You must enter life with all your being, why?
One simply cannot afford not to.
In this world, there has been so many why's.

147

Man must look deep into the soul of man.
This is not the kingdom it's cracked up to be.
One can't build bridges by burning them down.
The world goes around to make room for those
who wish to fight and those who love peace.
The Mark of the beast is eternity.

The birth of prejudice is the chicken on your back
that mirror you are looking at is cracked.
The world can barely see your face,
and the girl behind you is kissing your lover.
The face is a hundred split images
taken from a world you once knew.

I shall come upon you like a cold shower of rain.
I shall listen to your grievances
and work my way into your heart.
I won't be laughing when the world goes bust,
but you'll find me lurking in the crust
of your toasts – I'll be here when you get back

148

I have given my life to all of it.
I mean to the rolling stones
that stay in their place without a sound
walk slowly. On the ice, you may slip.
Let the world be all you are.
I have given my life to all of it.

There is nothing here to make us wish
that the world had not come along.
But it's here now, and the world
is now your father, perhaps your mother
coming around the bend. We can hear it and bend
before the world comes to a halt.

I drink to the future and the present
that made us what we are.
I am contented with a kiss.
Drink to evening dinners.
I think about all the laughter
and the countless times we said: I love you.

149

Dancing together brings memories back
between life and you and the muse.
I chose you. The muse comes back wearing a hat.
We enjoyed a soft, mature Petrus
in the crisp and enticing summer wind.
on the nose, we inhaled licorice,

and that of nutmeg, cinnamon, and chocolate.
Through the summer of your infectious smile.
I laughed at myself in that summer of youth, fate
gave us what we were searching for: the hope
of living life beyond the self.
We promised to say goodbye with a kiss.

Through the darkness, it speeds
eating leaves
before the hungry insects set in
I am the autumn leaf that kisses your shadow.
I wait until the morning breaks.
Then kissing the earth are the snowflakes.

150

I am long at waiting for the night.
Then the sunlight would come and cast
shadows over you, and I would chase him away
with roaring thunder and lightning.
I stood up for you and was counted
for you, I will go out fighting.

Let them know that I fought to keep you in my dreams
even if the world comes at you with anger
Inside, I laugh with love and turn the page
to see you as a caesura, a simile
and transform into something new.
The world will always come back for you.

For life is a fable that keeps
running on Broadway
and every time, it ends
with someone falling off the stage.
It's a dirty show with hopeless creeps
that find themselves hovering across the page.

151

Life is a fable that keeps.
It's a story of falling, struggling souls.
The night was off
and this guy who coughed
his lungs out.
Sometimes, I feel like an inconsolable soul.

surviving on the fringes
Like a fool, life laughs at me.
I belong to this wonder of time
confused about the third life with a mask
that will eventually crack
and see me as splintered glass

through the summer, I fall
and I rise again
like a curl of cigarette smoke
that disappears into building vents.
In the darkness, I make out your coat.
You were running. Did you pay your rent?

152

I walk around with poetry in my head.
Wild metaphors and incantations.
I can't sleep steady on the bed.
A phrase or an image wakes me.
Always at the stroke of midnight.
It's hard to get back to sleep.

There is always something in life to distress
you. But even ice cream melts in winter.
Please be kind to your guests
and try hard to make them laugh.
They will come back again
and bring you heartwarming gifts.

I am roaming still.
Footsteps I hear
It must be him. Willem, I mean
from chasing me, he gets a thrill.
God won't intervene.
For too much he has seen.

153

Already, He knows the outcome.
Or is He just a concept somebody
planted in my head?
I don't dare ask.
We all have a right
to wear a mask.

I can gather the summer wind again.
Fame is always acquired at the expense
of others. Observe the world with a keen
eye. Let laughter roam the skies,
and nothing will come back to haunt you.
Only, I suspect, the sweetness of life

by time's last note, a worm is in my coat,
But it won't stop me from crying for you
or turning my back on the world
on account of breathing life into you.
I am at the corner again searching for love,
waiting for me there must be a girl.

154

The world slowly goes by.
Pigeons flex the muscles of their wings
the last hour falls on the face of the sun
love of every object makes me sing
and to the world's horror, it won't run.
There is a mystery in everything – love.

In such times, love will go on right or wrong.
You will hear angels. The night
comes before us and settles there a song
that none of us understands.
Follow us throughout life.
It takes us all back to where we began.

Inside the trough of life, dead souls are waiting to be
washed with the oils of Christ.
The seasons she left us dry and low.
You couldn't say it was the last blow
from every object, living or dead
every man needs a slice.

155

Sometimes it's complicated knowing how to love.
Evil, somehow, finds its way in our path
of what we are is everything but death
who waits in the shadow of something else
from the theme of this pic I digress
into other worlds and images.

I will say to you that life is not a game.
Let's love and beloved for yesterday
are the brothers of tomorrow.
Do not dive into the pockets of fame.
Attention will bring you grief and sorrow.
Love, wherever you go, I will follow.

Now, look, I am stuck in time
with futile tasks to occupy what's left.
Of living in a world crawling with
dreams and angels. One must cross the line.
To see what's on the other side.
One has nowhere to go. One is confined.

156

To this horrid room that calls itself a world.
I exist without knowing what comes next.
Against the elements that make me. I fight.
There are so many yesterdays I do not remember
and doubtful about tomorrow.
From the beginning, the present had me fooled.

The future turned out to be a wrench
in the dwindling spokes of time.
Outside, a windless autumn dance around.
A ticking clock that provides no meaning
that the world will change; there is no change sign.
Living without meaning and seeming

Not to know what distant shadows drive me
towards you. I am the naked night that helps
you see the voice that causes you backward
toward an alternative world. Hence, what
age of life has taken you back to nothing?
I am the only fountain from which life comes.

157

I am the joy of heaven, the hope that you desire,
for inside the trough of life, there are dead souls
that roam the universe in search of nothing.
Time comes to you with hands outstretched
to help you along, but nothing is understood.
Only the silent song of whispering woods.

Taking you back to the beginning
where darkness and silence reigned.
But it won't be that. He sleeps under your hat
without any intention of waking.
He lays dormant like a virus
taking lives without a tinge of remorse.

Please let me fall,
and I shall rise again
to make love to you anew.
I shall rise again
thinking of you
embrace me. I shall greet you once more.

158

Come with me through the maze of scrambling objects.
Through the world I don't understand
along the path where no grass grows,
and I follow nothing but there are
only in that madness of flame.
I gather myself and give to you.

Behind it all was he
trying to explain what he was.
Besides sin and desire.
We didn't believe him.
He was a child playing with fire.
I suspect he had demons within.

I walk around with poetry in my head.
Wild metaphors and incantations.
I can't sleep steady on the bed.
A phrase or image wakes me.
Always at the stroke of midnight.
It's hard to get back to sleep.

159

I won't let empty pockets prevent us from wedding;
embrace the setting and let the laws fall
I'll come and get you when the time is right.
It will always be my call.
I won't ever let you fall.
Living life becomes the art of existence.

I kiss you now, for this is all that's left.
In silence, we both see the end
and death is not a friend.
It waits in every crevice of your life.
Sometimes, you'd see it coming
at other times, not.

But that has always been the plot.
By nothing else, I see
happiness, and sweetness are always in the slot,
and we should always relish it.
You have kept me going.
With you, I always want to sit.

160

Please let me fall
and I shall rise again
to make love to you again
to make love to you anew.
I am the rain clouds
that are still asleep
the weather, I repeat.

The stars did not mention that.
You'd be on my path.
But something was looking for you.
I don't know what it was.
Perhaps it was me that night
who followed you home.

At night, the voices came, and I heard yours,
and you were the pleasure of all that's sweet.
So sweet that it left under a spell.
In the summer your soul cling to mine,
and I found it difficult to tell
love, a subtle instinct, has no signs.

161

I have crossed the street.
But I didn't see you in the crowd.
My happiness for you is complete.
Our laughter and tears are in shreds
of confusion. Love has silenced me
in the arms of someone else.

But my heart beats only for you.
Let me walk you home. I'll sing you a song.
And kiss the violets that were your lips.
I don't know if to love you was right or wrong.
But to have seen the world as you see it
fulfilled me as one with you,

and on that night, I saw my ghost
that non-entity was breathing hard.
Why, he was dancing to the music.
He had great moves, too, that old bard.
He had the slow and fast two-step going.
I tried but I could not keep up with him.

162

Laughter, I suspect, is a tonic of the soul.
I no longer get delight in laughter.
I am confined to a life of solace in old age.
The youth of life has disappeared.
I am searching for the landscape of the page,
and I have slowly grown into a sage.

I have come forth into the night and seen
things I have not seen. In time, the world catches up.
But even at the crossroads, you continued
walking, unable to see what was under your boots.
The clouds began to gather, and the willows of the night
opened onto new worlds without people.

I have given all to love and lived the hard days
of winter, and my warmth was thoughts of you.
I remember those voices of youth
when your laughter piqued my heart.
I rambled on in love and other things.
I don't know if I was something at which to look.

163

But my heart was as warm as a fireplace
while those four walls were cold,
and I was only the image of you
that guaranteed my warmth for the summer
was far off. I lived with a life-threatening cough.
From love, I was never a runner.

I walk around with poetry in my head
wild metaphors and incantations.
I can't sleep steady on the bed.
A phrase or image wakes me.
Always at the stroke of midnight.
It's hard to get back to sleep.

Through the darkness, it speeds
eating leaves
before the hungry insects set in.
I am the autumn leaf that kisses your shadow
I wait until the morning breaks.
Then the snowflakes kiss the earth.

164

Leave a trail so I can find you. I start
at the beginning because it was something new.
Then at the ending of nothing else
the best of you were the worse of me.
It was you who held me hostage in a dream.
I was docile and not at all mean.

You were like a mother calling out to me.
I did not throw any temper tantrums.
We were getting to know each other again
This was at the end of the nuclear war.
Dead bodies were everywhere. We stood there
wondering what had gone wrong.

Unknown to us was these mushrooms sing.
We looked at each other and wondered why
God had spared us. We weren't special
What links us all in the autumn wind
is the rotten soul of man
that limps away in sin.

165

And he begged the world to drag you along.
Until death, everybody is strong.
We move inside flaps of the wind.
Listen to the vocals of Sarah Vaughn.
The summer wind helps us along.
Ella Fitzgerald awaits you.

I see poetry and jazz in dancing shoes.
In the autumn wind, the shadows fall,
and I find myself running back to you.
I searched for you while jazz played in the mall.
Life, sometimes, is a foolish concept.
Sit and listen to Coltrane's *Giant Steps.*

I walk around with poetry in my head,
wild metaphors and incantations
I can't sleep steady on the bed.
A phrase or an image wake me.
Always at the stroke of midnight.
It's hard to get back to sleep.

166

On the wake, feed me the guitar songs
Of West Montgomery and the piano
voice of Bill Evans. Put me to sleep with
the poetic voice of Eartha Kitt.
I see her before me, purring like a cat
and to her off, I take my hat.

Through the summer, I fell,
and your joy was intertwined with mine.
I can't imagine separation between us.
But love does not stall
because of a few fights about silly things.
Let's hold hands and cuddle.

I await that calmness that you bring.
So I wait for you in darkness and in light.
I feel anger at your leaving.
Only the mysterious crisscross of time
slipping, when I glanced back,
the needle did not move at all. We were all fooled.

167

Again, I will say to you life is not a game.
Let's love each other by the tide of yesterday
along time coming is the end of us
and I must tell you, all remain the same
unfortunately, it will hit us hard
that we will all die in the burning flames.

Our offspring will rise out of the ashes,
and life, with its sadness, will trundle on,
bringing the debris of the past with it.
From the flames, nothing will survive long.
It won't. Not in this volatile climate
where men, like sharks, are ready for each other.

Please let me fall
and I shall rise again
to make love to you anew.
I shall rise again
thinking of you
embrace me, and I shall greet you once more.

168

You will find the world between you and me
working its way to you.
I am the night forge into nothingness.
You became the spotlight on my darkness.
Sometimes I descend into a world I cannot see
swing by the shadow of eternity.

Through the darkness it speeds
eating leaves
before the hungry insects set in.
I am the autumn leaf that kisses your shadow.
I wait until the morning breaks.
Then the snowflakes kiss the earth.

I am the poetic dream of a life you once had.
I am the sentinel of all things.
So, some with me for I am that.
Let me pass for poetry is my guard
that I remember your only star
is my kiss and loyalty to the heart.

169

Bring me home, let me see you at the window.
The sunlight waits for you.
I'll wait for you.
The days wane with life.
Before all else, get to the meaning
of every object,

and where, in time, you seem
not to care that life has got you in a bind.
Of all the laughter we have enjoyed,
everything always seems to end in tears.
You'd be standing while I seem to fall.
The thing with balance is not my game.
Neither is the preoccupation with fame.

Please let me fall,
and I shall rise again
to make love to you anew.
I shall rise again
thinking of you.
Embrace me, and I shall greet you once more.

170

Poetry is the life blood of what I am.
It's the origin of the word
gist of the metaphor
and the elusive dream
of the caesura.
You are the smiling face of the simile.

I walk around with poetry in my head
wild metaphors and incantations.
I can't sleep steady in the bed.
A phrase or an image wakes me.
Always at the stroke of midnight.
It's hard to get back to sleep.

The world has become what it is.
Objects lay dormant, and nobody
can tell what they are. Within them
lies the secret of all that is new.
I have seen the angels fall.
But none has yet revealed the secret.

171

Of what life is intended to mean.
All in all, the world is seeming not to seem.
It does not reveal itself to us,
It casts its own shadow where the land
is fertile and stretches beyond nothing.
People, like zombies, roam the streets.

Political structures have collapsed.
A dark and evil cloud floats across the fields
and the ghosts hover about our heads.
There is nothing in the world to see now.
But the afterflames of a burning world.
At the end of it, you will see a girl.

Her face will be a fickle half smile,
a look languid with a false expression.
We have all been stamped and filed
under the mysterious John Doe,
a figure we now know is each of us.
Above us, the clouds are heavy with rain.

172

I walk around with poetry in my head,
wild metaphors and incantations.
I can't sleep steady on the bed.
A phrase or an image wakes me.
Always on the stroke of midnight.
It's hard to get back to sleep.

Unfortunately, we are out of frame
dawn and deadbeat to the tune of despair.
I hear nothing of you. Only the dark voice
and if we had been given that choice.
I suspect that life would be the same.
We all know it has always been God's game.

There is no escape. The trap has been set
and nobody had eyes to see it.
Lucifer was sitting on the sidelines.
To him, it was a joke. He was laughing.
It was not at all beyond him.
The night of all sin was his fictitious game.

173

We are the evil of what we are
and the burden of every star.
For each of us, a space is vacant,
and in it is our resting place.
It will always be waiting there
behind all else, the moonlight slips.

The clouds are scattered now as if to make
room for us, we will see the end.
But will never understand it. It flips
us to one side, and with fate, we collide
asking nothing of ourselves but to dance
with what is left of two opposite poles.

I crossed the street at a green light
but did not see you in the crowd.
You must have slipped through some reversed portal
that rendered you invisible.
I walked on ahead, thinking that
you were still in the crowd. Then I glanced over my shoulder; they
were